REVISED

WATER

Words by Harlan Wade

Concept and illustrations by
Denis Wrigley

RAINTREE CHILDRENS BOOKS
Milwaukee · Toronto · Melbourne · London

Library of Congress Number: 78-21290

1 2 3 4 5 6 7 8 9 0 83 82 81 80 79

Printed in the United States of America.

Library of Congress Cataloging in Publication Data

Wade, Harlan.
  Water.

  (His A book about)
  SUMMARY: Explains the basic properties and uses
of water.
    1. Water—Juvenile literature. [1. Water]
I. Wrigley, Denis. II. Title. III. Series.
GB662.3.W33 1979   553′7   78-21290
ISBN 0-8172-1539-5 lib. bdg.

WATER

What do you know
about water?

It is wet!

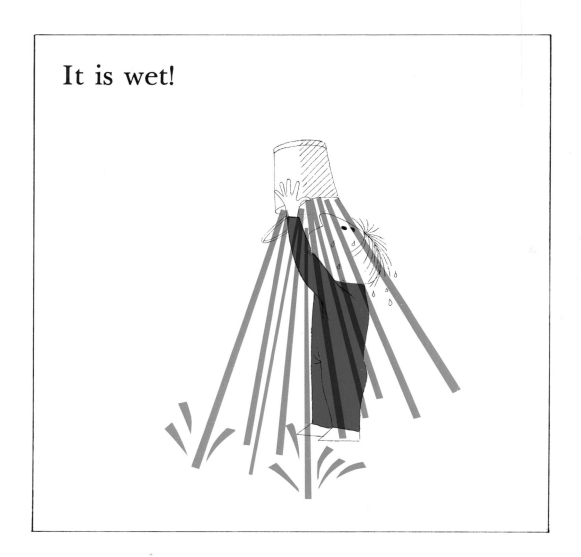

You can't hold on to water.
It won't stay in one shape.
It flows.

Water is clear. You can see through it.

9

When water boils,
it turns to steam.

When water freezes,
it turns to ice.

Some things can stay on top of water. We call this floating.

Look around. You can find water in many places.

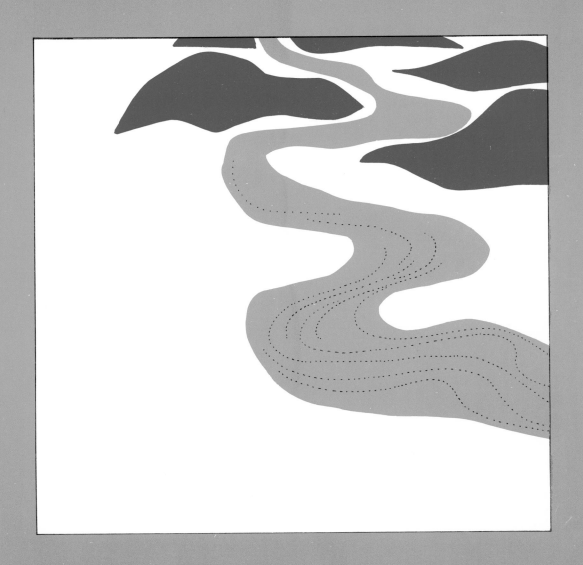

15

The sea is water.

So are lakes.

Rain is water too.

Fruit juice is mostly water.

And so are tears.

Water can be used
in many ways.

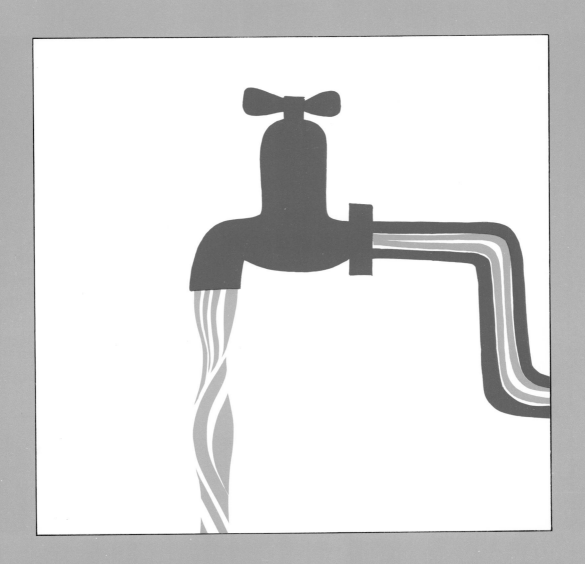

23

Water washes.

We can drink water. We can mix it with other things.

Water can move things.
We call this waterpower.

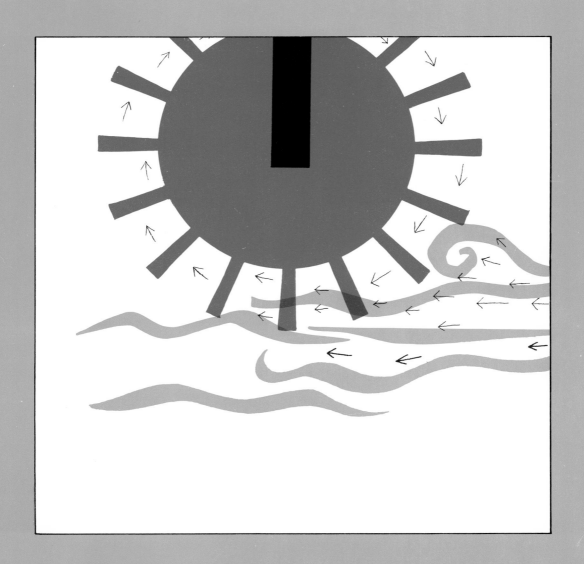

Some animals live in water
all the time.

29

All living things need water to live.

We wish to thank Mr. Glen Burk, Principal,
Wisconsin Avenue School, Milwaukee, Wisconsin,
for his assistance. We would also like to thank
Mrs. Gardenia Limehouse and her third grade class
and Mrs. Camille Maduscha and her second grade class
for reading some of the books in this series
and sharing their comments with us.

Erica, age 8 — "It's good."
Larry, age 8 — "The story tells a lot."
LeVaughn, age 8 — "It's a funny book."
Alphonso, age 8 — "I like the way it looks."
Nicole, age 7 — "I would like to take it home."
Pete, age 8 — "The book is easy for me to read."
Steven, age 8 — "I like the information in the book."